# Key Stage 2 of the National Curriculum

## INTRODUCTION

It is Daniel's first day at junior school. The school yard is full of children aged between seven and eleven. Daniel is seven, so it is his first day in Year 3. It's a funny feeling to be one of the youngest children in the school, because only six weeks ago, when he left the infants' school just down the road, he was one of the top dogs, one of the 'big children in Year 2' that the head teacher always said had set such a good example to the younger classes. Now, in his new junior school, he is one of the younger children again.

There are a few differences when he thinks back to his infant school. The furniture is bigger, but he was getting too tall for those little chairs anyway, so he is glad about that. He's a bit worried, however, because there are more men teachers. In his infant school all the teachers were women, so he's not had a man teacher before. But he doesn't worry for long, because Mr Westwood, his class teacher, tells them they will enjoy Year 3, and he will only get cross with them if they start acting silly.

What about Daniel's curriculum? Well fortunately it just carries on from where he left off in his infant school. Daniel has now completed the first phase of the National Curriculum, Key Stage 1, which is for five to seven year olds, and he is about to start the second phase, Key Stage 2, aimed at seven to eleven year olds. All the subjects are exactly the same – the three core subjects, English, Maths and Science for quite a lot of the week, and the six foundation subjects, Art, Geography, History, Music, Physical Education and Technology as well.

'Will we be doing any projects?' Daniel asks, because he liked the projects they did in the infant school. Mr Westwood tells him that they will have lessons on all the subjects, but they will also be doing some big projects. One will be called 'The Romans', which sounds as if it is only about history, but the way Mr Westwood does it there will be a lot more besides. Daniel doesn't know it yet, but in the summer term the class will be going to the city of Bath to see the Roman baths. They will also be dressing up as Romans and making up a play about the Romans in Britain, so that will help them in their English lessons. There will also be some Geography (where and how the Romans lived, what lands they conquered), Art (drawing and painting pictures for their wall display), and Technology (things the Romans invented, used and built).

Daniel is already quite a good reader for his age, so he will enjoy 'reading time' when children in Year 3 go to the library to choose a book they want to read. Mr Westwood likes his class to take their books home and talk to their parents about them. In fact, Daniel will find that he gets quite a bit more responsibility for organizing himself, now that he is older and bigger. Key Stage 2 is going to be a vital time in his education, because he should make rapid progress between seven and

*If you're going to be silly I'll get cross*

eleven, when he will grow from a little child, just out of infant school, into a near adolescent, ready for secondary school.

This *Guide to Key Stage 2* covers the important years from the age of seven up to eleven. During this time children will go to some form of primary school, often the same one they attended between the ages of five and seven, sometimes the sister junior school of the infant school they used to go to. At the end of their infant school days they will have finished the first of the four phases of the National Curriculum, known as 'Key Stages', so they are now ready to move on to the second phase, known as 'Key Stage 2'. The other three Key Stages are covered in other books in this series.

For parents faced with finding a new school when their child is seven, the *Guide to Key Stage 1* in this series has a special section on choosing a primary school.

**The four Key Stages of the National Curriculum**

Key Stage 1 is from 5 to 7
**Key Stage 2 is from 7 to 11**
Key Stage 3 is from 11 to 14
Key Stage 4 is from 14 to 16

## STARTING KEY STAGE 2

Seven year olds like Daniel already have two to three years of schooling under their belt, so they should have acquired some of the basic knowledge and skills they will need in the next four years of their education. Most seven year olds have made a significant start on reading and are able to read simple books on their own, making an intelligent guess at words they don't know. They ought to be able to write simple sentences, using capital letters and full stops, in neat legible handwriting, spelling the short words correctly.

They should also have a grasp of basic concepts in Mathematics and Science, be able to add and subtract, use words like 'rectangle' and 'triangle' to describe shapes, carry out a simple experiment, know what plants and animals need to keep them alive and what sort of use is made of electricity. In addition to the three core subjects, English, Maths and Science, seven year olds will have done two or three years work in the other six subjects in the National Curriculum, so they should be ready to move on to higher levels.

In the perfect world of washing-up liquid and breakfast cereal adverts, Daniel will have been a model pupil, sailing brilliantly through his infant school and entering junior school with a flying start. In the real world, of course, he might have day-dreamed his life away in class, fallen behind with his reading and sent both his parents and teacher up the wall. Either way his junior school should help him to build on what he has learned in the first phase of the National Curriculum, getting him back on track if necessary.

Seven to eleven year olds are at what is sometimes called the 'concrete' stage of development. They like to see specific examples and learn though personal experience, rather than study in a more theoretical or abstract way. In Geography a teacher might talk to them about 'housing', but they would probably learn more if they also went round their town looking at housing in the area, and saw films and photographs of houses in many different places. Quite a lot of Daniel's curriculum, therefore, will involve practical work, activities and personal experience.

## HOW SCHOOL IS ORGANISED

Between the ages of seven and eleven children usually attend a *junior* or *middle* school. In many cases, especially in rural areas, they will go to an all-age *primary* school that might take children for the whole of the period from age five up to eleven, or even twelve. Most schools nowadays number the classes by year group, following on from the infant stage, during Key Stage 2 of the National Curriculum.

Seven year olds will have just left their Year 2 class, so the newcomers to Key Stage 2 will start in Year 3.

A simple way of remembering how old children are in any year group is to add five, the starting age of schooling, to the number. If someone says, 'year 6 will be doing national tests next week' this means that the children in that class will reach the age of eleven during the school year. If you had three children who would be aged eight, ten and thirteen by August, then they would probably be in Year 3, Year 5 and Year 8, because the numbering system carries on right through primary and secondary school.

### How old are children in each class during Key Stage 2?

| | |
|---|---|
| Year 3 | 7–8 year olds |
| Year 4 | 8–9 year olds |
| Year 5 | 9–10 year olds |
| Year 6 | 10–11 year olds |

As in the infant school or early years stage of schooling it is common for pupils to stay in the same class each day with their 'class teacher'. There might be a bit of 'specialist' teaching in some junior schools, perhaps in subjects like Music, Science or Physical Education, when someone other than the class teacher takes the group. This is more likely to happen near the top of the primary school to help prepare children for secondary schools when they might have nine or ten different teachers.

## WHAT DO CHILDREN LEARN BETWEEN SEVEN AND ELEVEN?

With so much *knowledge* available in our society no one, not even the finest minds in the world, can know more than a fraction of what is in the millions of books, reports and journals available today. Children now aged seven to eleven will still be at school when the twenty-first century dawns. It is difficult to guess what sort of jobs they will do (or even if they will have a job at all in the next century), but they may have to retrain several times, and with luck they will enjoy 30 years or more of healthy retirement.

Children in primary schools need to develop their *whole personality*, so that important personal qualities like determination, curiosity, imagination and flexibility can flourish, especially if they are to be able to adapt to changing circumstances. One purpose of the *curriculum* of a school is to develop the subject knowledge, personal and social qualities children are going to need as adults of the future.

We have had a National Curriculum in England and Wales since 1988. It was simplified in 1995, and for the 1998–2000 period it was modified again for primary schools. English, Maths, Science and Information Technology remained the same, and a daily literacy and numeracy hour were introduced. Teachers still had to teach the other subjects, but were allowed to reduce the content of them.

*Technology – one of the foundation subjects at Key Stage 2*

The National Curriculum is a curriculum that schools must teach by law, and children start to study it from the moment they first enter school at the age of five, until they reach the age of sixteen. It consists of nine subjects. Three – English, Maths and Science – are known as the *core subjects* and the other six – Art, Geography, History, Music, Physical Education and Technology – are called the *foundation subjects*.

In addition all children have had to study Religious Education by law since the 1944 Education Act. A Modern Language is not required until children start secondary school. In Wales children also learn Welsh as a core subject in areas where Welsh is spoken, while in non-Welsh speaking schools it is a foundation subject.

| Core subjects | Foundation subjects |
|---|---|
| | Art |
| English | Geography |
| | History |
| Mathematics | Music |
| | Physical Education |
| Science | Technology |

**TABLE 1  The subjects of the National Curriculum at Key Stage 2**

## NATIONAL CURRICULUM – LEARNING THE JARGON

By the time their children are seven many parents may have learned a little 'Advanced Martian', as the language of the National Curriculum is sometimes known. There are a few terms that are worth knowing so you can bluff your way through conversations about education, and these include the following:

### Programmes of Study (PoS)

In a subject like Mathematics, what children study between the ages of seven and eleven is mapped out under four main headings:

1.  Using and Applying Mathematics
2.  Number
3.  Shape, Space and Measures
4.  Handling Data

These National Curriculum *Programmes of Study* spell out the detail of what children will actually learn. So children aged seven to eleven doing Mathematics under the second heading, *Number*, will learn about several aspects, including the following:

- *the number system* understand decimals, fractions, percentages, negative numbers;
- *relationships between numbers* consolidate multiplication up to $10 \times 10$, squares and square roots, proportions, mental estimation, use of the different functions on a calculator, like memories, constants and brackets;
- *solving problems* choosing appropriate methods, like the use of spreadsheets, checking, estimating, selecting an appropriate degree of accuracy.

### Attainment Targets (ATs)

Many of the National Curriculum subjects that children study in primary school have what are called *Attainment Targets*. These are statements about what children will achieve at different stages of the various aspects of the subject being studied. The core subject English, for example, has three Programmes of Study and three corresponding sets of Attainment Targets. Number 1 is 'Speaking and Listening', number 2 is 'Reading' and number 3 is 'Writing' (including handwriting and spelling). The term 'Attainment Target' is often abbreviated to *AT*, so 'Speaking and Listening' is AT1 and 'Writing' is AT3. When children are eleven and have reached the end of this phase of the National Curriculum, their writing should show the following:

- a range of forms of written work, done in a lively and thoughtful way;
- ideas sustained and developed and organized appropriately for the purpose and reader;
- good vocabulary and ability to construct grammatically complex sentences;
- spelling generally accurate, of both shorter and longer words;
- correct use of full stops, capital letters, question marks and other punctuation;
- handwriting fluent, joined up and legible.

This represents the achievement of an average eleven year old at Level 4 (see below).

## Levels

Progress through the National Curriculum is recorded on a scale with eight different *Levels* in all the subjects except Art, Music and Physical Education. Level 1 is the first stage at which five year olds begin their work. As children advance through the National Curriculum they will move from one Level up to the next, both in primary and secondary schools, as the scale goes on up to the age of fourteen. In primary school children will cover the first four or five of the Levels, and the average seven year old starts junior school at Level 2. By the end of primary education the average eleven year old will have reached Level 4.

In practice children of the same age will be spread across several levels. When they start Key Stage 2 at the age of seven about a quarter of them are still on Level 1, roughly half are on Level 2, and another quarter are on Level 3. A few children have not yet reached Level 1, and a very small number are on Level 4. By the end of Key Stage 2, four years later, eleven year olds are even more widely spread, and although the average child will be at Level 4, some may still be operating at Level 2, while those who have made most progress may have reached as high as Level 6.

| Average ability at age | Level |
| --- | --- |
| 7 | 2 |
| 11 | 4 |

TABLE 2   Average level reached by children at the beginning and at the end of Key Stage 2

## QUESTION TIME

### Is the National Curriculum at Key Stage 2 very different from Key Stage 1?

Yes and no. The subjects, English, Maths, Science and so on, are the same, but some of them introduce brand new topics. In Maths, for example, there were three Programmes of Study at Key Stage 1, but at Key Stage 2 a fourth one is introduced. It is called 'Handling Data', and it covers graphs, statistics, pie charts and other means of dealing with mathematical information.

### Does the National Curriculum lay down what teachers must do at Key Stage 2?

No. As was the case in Key Stage 1, the teaching methods are decided by the teachers, though to some extent *how* they teach will be determined by *what* they have to teach. In Science, for example, children are expected to learn about magnets. In order to find out what kinds of materials magnets will and will not pick up, or what happens when two magnets are pushed together, teachers will have to give pupils the opportunity to do the necessary practical work. There has, however, been strong government pressure on teachers to follow official guidelines on how the daily literacy hour and numeracy hour should be taught.

### Do children study each subject in the National Curriculum separately at Key Stage 2?

No. As was the case in Key Stage 1, individual schools can decide what they will teach separately and what through projects and topics covering more than one subject. The law on the National Curriculum only says what must be taught. It does not lay down whether Science can ever be combined with Technology. Most teachers of seven to eleven year olds will try to cover certain *themes* as well as individual *subjects*. They might tackle a topic like *Energy*, which could cover several subjects. These could include Science (forces, electricity, solar power), Maths (how energy is measured), Technology (how machines get, store and use energy), Geography (what power resources are available to us and where they come from – coal, oil, electricity, gas), History (comparing energy available in homes in Victorian Britain with homes today – cooking, heating, lighting, machinery), English (reading, writing and speaking about energy), Art (drawing and painting scenes related to a visit to a power station, for example).

*Today's topic is energy ...*

## THE THREE CORE SUBJECTS

By the age of seven most children have made a decent start on what are sometimes called the 'basics'. The basics are much wider than they once were, as Science is a central part of them. Nowadays it is not so much a matter of children learning the three Rs, it is more like at least four, if you include Science – reading, 'riting,

'rithmetic and 'ruddy 'ell, Nora, I don't understand a word of what he's on about'. In junior school much of the school week is spent on the three core subjects, English, Maths and Science, and children have to cover quite a bit of ground between the ages of five and seven.

*Remember!* The programmes described below are what children do between seven and eleven, so seven and eight year olds will only be making a start on them. There is not space to reproduce the whole curriculum, so examples are given.

**ENGLISH**     By the time they reach the age of seven most children have quite a good command of spoken English, with a vocabulary of many thousands of words. They will, in most cases, also have made a significant start on reading and writing. Most adults would be delighted to be able to speak, read and write Japanese or Russian as well as the average seven year old handles English. We know that we could more than survive in the country concerned. Once children enter the second phase of the National Curriculum they begin to extend their language even further. In English they have three Programmes of Study that should help this development considerably. These three are exactly the same as in Key Stage 1:

1.  Speaking and Listening
2.  Reading
3.  Writing

The three areas may be tackled separately or in combination. There is supposed to be a daily literacy hour, consisting roughly of half an hour of whole class teaching, looking at texts and studying words and sentences, followed by twenty minutes of individual and group work, and ten minutes of review. This pattern is voluntary, but there has been strong pressure on teachers to follow it.

### Speaking and Listening

It is always funny when schools have a sponsored silence. The longer the children keep their mouths shut, the more money they raise for charity or for school funds. It is often a mighty relief for teachers and parents to have a blissful silence instead of the chatter of high-pitched voices. But it is a good job these sponsored silences are usually short lived. If they went on too long, then children would find it hard to meet the requirements of the 'Speaking and Listening' programme, for here are a few of the things children are supposed to do at this stage of their education:

■  explore, develop and clarify their own ideas, expressing them clearly and confidently;

■  plan, predict, investigate and organize what they want to say;

■  read aloud, tell and enact stories and poems;

■  listen carefully to what people say, including on radio and television programmes, and be able to question others about their ideas;

■  take part in drama, including improvization, role-play, and the writing and performing of scripted drama.

It is not exactly a programme for Trappist monks. There is considerable emphasis on children learning Standard English and being able to tell the difference between this and dialects. This is not quite the same as *regional accents*. Standard English is the so-called 'correct' form of the language, whereas a regional accent is the way people in different places actually pronounce the words. 'He don't look roight 'appy to me' is West Country dialect, whereas 'That answer is not roight' is Standard English spoken with a West Country accent.

During their four years in this phase of education children will also be encouraged to broaden their vocabulary, using more adventurous and imaginative words. This was neatly demonstrated in one class of eight and nine year olds I watched. The teacher asked the class what it would be like to visit a big, dark forest, and then skilfully helped extend their vocabulary as different pupils answered:

| | |
|---|---|
| *Pupil* | Spooky and creepy. |
| *Teacher* | Better than 'spooky and creepy'? |
| *Pupil* | Strange and weird. |
| *Teacher* | Yes, 'strange and weird'. How about a word beginning with two e's? Do you know it? |
| *Pupil* | Eerie. |
| *Teacher* | Yes. What does 'eerie' mean? |
| *Pupil* | Scary. |

Choosing the most appropriate words and expressions according to the person or people you are addressing is also an important feature. 'Cheers, Mike', is a common way of saying goodbye to a close friend, but 'Cheers, Bish', would not sound quite right when leaving the Archbishop of Canterbury.

## Reading

Although many seven year olds will already have read several simple stories and different kinds of non-fiction books, some may not have made such good progress. During this phase of their education schools need to make sure that those children who are not as far advanced as the others can catch up as quickly as possible. They will also need to help pupils develop what are sometimes called the 'higher skills of reading'.

Many adults have to read a great deal, both in their jobs and at home. To help them cope with this increased amount of reading they have often developed skills they don't even think about, like the ability to skim quickly, to slow down when they get to the hard or important bits, to make notes, to pick out the key points in a document. Between the ages of seven and eleven children need to acquire these higher skills of reading.

Reading at this age involves children reading a much wider range of literature than they could have tackled in infant school. 'Ancient and modern' is the general message. They should learn to read critically, not just believe blindly that everything they see in print is the truth, and their reading should cover the following:

- modern fiction by significant children's authors;
- long-established children's fiction;
- good quality modern poetry;
- classic poetry;
- texts from different cultures and traditions;
- myths, legends and traditional stories.